D1278024

Little Pebble™

Our Families

Brothers
Are Part of a Family

by Lucia Raatma

CAPSTONE PRESS
a capstone imprint

Little Pebble is published by Capstone Press,
1710 Roe Crest Drive, North Mankato, Minnesota 56003
www.mycapstone.com

**Library of Congress Cataloging-in-Publication Data is available
on the Library of Congress website**

ISBN: 978-1-5157-7461-7 (library binding)
ISBN: 978-1-5157-7471-6 (paperback)
written by Lucia Raatma

Editorial Credits
Christianne Jones, editor; Juliette Peters, designer;
Wanda Winch, media researcher; Laura Manthe, production specialist

Photo Credits
Capstone Studio: Karon Dubke, 7, 11, 13, 15, 19, 21; Shutterstock: Angelina Babii,
paper texture, atikinka, cover, Jaren Jai Wicklund, 5, Lisa F. Young, 1, littlekidmoment, 17,
Romrodphoto, 9, Teguh Mujiono, tree design

Printed and bound in China.
010428F17

Table of Contents

Brothers

A brother may have sisters.

He may also have brothers.

They are family.

Rob has a brother.

Rob's brother is a toddler.

Jack has a brother.
They were born on the
same day. They are twins.

Liz has a brother.

He is older than Liz.

What Brothers Do

Michael likes books.

He reads with his sister.

Max has a brother.

They help with chores.

Harry likes to play with his brother. They like the water.

Wilson's sister needs help. Wilson helps her tie her shoe.

Brothers laugh.

They play.

They are pals.

Glossary

brother—a boy who has the same parents as another person

family—a group of people related to one another

sister—a girl who has the same parents as another person

toddler—a young child who just learned to walk

twin—one of two children born at the same time to the same parents

Read More

Harris, Robie H. *Who's in My Family? All About Our Families.* Somerville, MA: Candlewick, 2012.

Hunter, Nick. *Finding Out About Your Family History.* Mankato, MN: Heinemann-Raintree, 2015.

Lewis, Clare. *Familes Around the World.* Mankato, MN: Heinemann-Raintree, 2015.

Internet Sites

FactHound offers a safe, fun way to find Internet sites related to this book. All of the sites on FactHound have been researched by our staff.

Here's all you do:
Visit *www.facthound.com*
Type in this code: 9781515774617

Check out projects, games and lots more at
www.capstonekids.com

Index